THE TOTAL
JESUS

WHY PROTESTANTS ONLY GET HALF OF JESUS!

Dr. Paul J. Young

THE TOTAL
JESUS

Dr. Paul J. Young

Read This First

No one discards a box of delicious fried chicken because it has bones. No way! You grab a piece, eat the meat and discard the bones.

So too with this book. Eat the meat - there is a lot here to chew on, think about, process and pray about. If you find any bones, discard them. Why waste all the meat because there are a few bones!

No book authored by a human is perfect, you know. We seek to write about infinite truth with only a finite understanding using a finite, limited language. I speak what I know has been revealed as accurately as possible without swerving to the left or right of the truth.

And that's it, isn't it - TRUTH.

I trust you find much in this book that will arrest your attention, and that you will line yourself with what is true, for the betterment of your soul.

There is no better way.

There is so much more that can be written. This book will not cover all the issues in depth. I encourage you, as you seek answers to do further, in-depth study. Books for further study are listed at the end of this book.[1]

I did not find anything heretical in the book. You spoke to the average person in a very clear and passionate way. It is a good book for those seeking the truth of the Eucharist.

Comment from a trusted Catholic Priest and friend

---

[1] Read Catholic apologist David Armstrong, connect with Catholic Answers at catholic.com, or reach out to The Coming Home Network (chnetwork.org) where a few thousand Protestant pastors have become Catholic along with thousands of lay people, fully committed to Jesus Christ as Lord and Savior.

Table Of Contents

1

Why I Had To Write This Book

During the days of Covid 19, many churches were closed with ministry only occurring over the internet, thus internet churches that were effective and, at least in part, filled in the gap of no church at all.

Protestant friends of mine did not like not going to church, but big deal, they could still listen to their pastor give his weekly sermon. And that was good enough.

But not for Catholics!

You see,
Catholics go to Church
not just to listen to a sermon or homily
Or even to be with their friends
but
TO RECEIVE JESUS CHRIST -

His Flesh and Blood, Soul and Divinity.

You can't do that on the internet!

It was during this time of spiritual starvation
for the Flesh and Blood of Christ
that I thought of this book - the importance of the
Eucharist

The NECESSITY of the Eucharist!
And that Protestants miss out on
The TOTAL JESUS.

So, with this necessity in mind and the contrast
between what Protestants receive in their church
service and what a Catholic receives, I HAD TO
WRITE THIS BOOK. I felt a strong urging from the
Holy Spirit to lay out the GREAT DIFFERENCE
between Protestants and Catholics - the fact that
Protestants only receive ½ of Jesus.

Incredible?

I believe that you will find the evidence I use will
be compelling - a view that hopefully will drive
you, if you are a Protestant, to receive the TOTAL
JESUS. And if you are a Catholic, to thank God for
the privilege of receiving this TOTAL Christ.

As Catholics who could not go to Mass during the Covid 19 crisis, but attended online, we prayed:

My Jesus

I believe
that you are present
in the most Holy Eucharist.

I love
you above all things, and

I desire
to receive you into my soul. Since

I cannot
at this moment
receive you sacramentally.
Come at least spiritually into my
heart.

I embrace
you as if you were already there
and unite myself wholly to you.
Never permit me to be separated from you.

Amen.

2

The BIG Question

TOTAL. LOOK IT UP IN THE DICTIONARY. It's pretty clear when we speak of total as to the meaning. There is no getting around it when I write about the TOTAL JESUS.

TOTAL.

How can you miss it?

Total means: absolute, entire, full, unrestricted, perfect, whole, true, real, substantial and undivided.

So when I write about the TOTAL JESUS, I am speaking about all of him, nothing short, nothing more or nothing less. Just JESUS in all he is.

How is it then that Protestants only get half of Jesus? Isn't that a little disparaging?

How arrogant, you say!

Who do these Catholics think they are by claiming they get all of Jesus when Protestants only get half of him.

How did they ever arrive at that conclusion? And...what do they use to support these claims?

Great questions.

I have a lot to cover in this book, a book that will hopefully peak your attention on this very important subject.

3

Protestants Only Receive Half Of Jesus

HOW RIDICULOUS - PROTESTANTS ONLY RECEIVING HALF OF JESUS, you say! At least this charge seems that way. What do I mean that Protestants get only half of Jesus.

"Which half," you say?

I am not talking about dividing his body - the right side or the left, the upper or the lower. Instead, as I am sure some of you have already guessed, I am talking about the TWO PARTS of Jesus.

"Two parts," you say?

For all of eternity Jesus was a PURE SPIRIT along with his Father and the Holy Spirit. Then, through the eternal plan of the Father, Jesus became man - Spirit and FLESH.

All Catholics and Protestants believe this awesome truth supported by some of the great Councils of the Church as well as Holy Scripture. We all, Catholics and Protestants, place our hope in the INCARNATION of Christ - God becoming man.

How could he die for us if he didn't have a body?

So if Protestants believe this, why am I saying that they only get half of Jesus?[2]

Now I could be wrong. You as a Protestant may have 60% or even 90% of Jesus when you believe and are baptized. Yet, you DON'T GET ALL OF HIM because you are not receiving the TOTAL JESUS. I am convinced of that.

And let me say that there is nothing in the Bible or in Catholic dogma that states that Protestants get only half of Jesus. If so, why am I suggesting it? You may think that I am crazy! Well, it's a little strange to talk about receiving only ½ of Jesus. Yet,

---

[2] I am not saying that they are not fully Christians. Through faith and baptism all are joined to Christ (Protestants and Catholics) and are full fledged members of his body. Then why make an issue regarding the Eucharist? I am not making the issue. Jesus is. He states clearly that all Christians need to eat his FLESH and drink his BLOOD. To receive Jesus the God and not Jesus the Man means that one only receives ½ of Jesus.

what if I have a point, what if, as a Protestant, you don't receive all of him?

WHAT IF?

If there is any truth in what I say, it's best you continue reading.

Stay with me.

Let me build the case slowly.

4

Jesus Is Not Just A Spirit

IN THE APOSTLES CREED WE SAY:

*I believe in God the **Father**...and in Jesus Christ his **Son** WHO WAS CONCEIVED BY THE HOLY SPIRIT, BORN OF THE VIRGIN MARY...I believe in the **Holy Spirit**...*

In this simple statement of belief we see that God the Father nor the Holy Spirit were ever incarnated in the flesh. It's kind of obvious, isn't it? They are pure SPIRITS.

St. John states that:

God is a SPIRIT and they that worship him must worship him in SPIRIT and in TRUTH.
                                              John 4

So we know that God is a SPIRIT. There is no question here. Yet, in the Trinity, God the Son IS MORE THAN A SPIRIT. Why? St. John says it clearly:

And the WORD (Jesus) **BECAME FLESH** *AND DWELT AMONG US and we beheld his glory…*

John 1

We see clearly that Jesus Christ, our Lord, is not just a Spirit but also FLESH. Because of this we can say:

God the Father - is a Spirit
God the Holy Spirit - is a Spirit
God the Son - is a Spirit and FLESH

Thus Jesus is FULLY God and FULLY human. Christ's body was totally, fully, purely human - God made flesh in the incarnation.

Early on in the formation of Christianity the gnostics wanted to deny that God took upon himself FLESH in his Son, Jesus Christ. They thought that flesh was evil - material would somehow lessen the purity of God. So they ultimately had to deny the incarnation of God and taught that Jesus was a lesser being.

The key I want to point out is that gnostics put ALL THEIR FOCUS ON THE SPIRIT. The SPIRIT was what was important. FLESH and the material world were passing away. The SPIRIT was what would last forever.

Yet this belief of the gnostics goes against the Hebrew Scriptures in the creation account where God said of the material world and all of his creation,

It is good!

The Scriptures says in Genesis 1 - 2, that creation was good 5 times and very good 1 time. This means that the material world that God created was exactly as God wanted coming from his powerful and perfect hands as he spoke creation into existence.

Material is good.

This is NOT saying that materialism is good. The Websters Dictionary defines materialism as…

a theory that physical matter is the only or fundamental reality

In other words: Matter is everything.

So in response to that, too many Protestants develop subtle gnostic attitudes about matter that somehow restricts God and his work.

Often I have heard them declare that they will be thrilled to get rid of their material body - a body that has chained them to this material, dark and evil world. They want liberation of their spirit.

Sounds good, doesn't it?

Yet they do not realize that when God made humans, he made them both material and spiritual, breathing his life and likeness into them so they could become living SOULS.

To be without your body is not a good thing. To be a soul is to be both material and immaterial - forever.

The body is not, as in some older ideas held, a mere hindrance to the soul, from whence the tradition of speaking of the soul may have come, but they are partners. And if the body becomes a hindrance to the spiritual progress of the person, it is not the body's fault, it is the fault of the whole person, who, either voluntarily, or through laziness, did not seek the union with the beloved.

St. John of the Cross

Christians after death will not be left "naked" without a body to live in.

For while we are in this body, we groan and are burdened, because we do not wish to be unclothed or bodiless, but to be clothed instead with our heavenly body - from the mortal to the immortal body.
2 Corinthians 5:3

Even after death, the immaterial part of you waits for the resurrection of your body - the corruptible body (See I Corinthians 15:15 - 58), that body that has been impacted by sin which will be raised an incorruptible, perfect body - flesh that is not fallen, having a bloodline tainted by sin. We will be souls that are perfect, FLESH AND SPIRIT - bodies just like Christ.

23

We are citizens of the high heaven who wait for our Savior, our Master, Jesus Christ who, when he comes, will transform our earthly, bodies of flesh into glorious, bodies of flesh like his own. He will make us absolutely beautiful and whole again. What power and skill he has!

Philippians 3:21

What a day that will be!

And get this. We will not be just SPIRITS, but like Jesus, FLESH (a body that is touchable, a body that can eat and enjoy pleasures that bodies are made to enjoy) and SPIRIT - all making up our souls.

This is what our Savior is. He is not just a Spirit. He is both material and immaterial, God incarnated (made FLESH) in a human body. And he will be that forever. His body was not just a temporary thing. The FLESH of Jesus was and is permanent.

So if we are going to fully receive Christ as our Lord and Savior, we need to receive him as he is - God and Man, Spirit and Flesh, all of him...The TOTAL JESUS.

How do we do this? How can we be connected to this Jesus who left the glories of heaven and became man, to live, love and die for each of us on the cross? How to we get the TOTAL JESUS?

Great question.

Keep reading.

5

The Sacraments And The Material World

THOUGH SOME PROTESTANTS USE THE TERM "SACRAMENT," most don't.

Lutherans, Episcopalians, Anglicans and a few other groups refer to baptism, and the Eucharist as Sacraments, whereas Baptists (the Southern Baptist being the largest Protestant denomination) and most Evangelicals see baptism and communion as symbols only.

They give no value to the material aspect to water (baptism), to bread and wine (Eucharist), and to the other physical, material aspects that make up a Sacrament (material and spiritual tied together).[3] Dr. J. Vernon McGee[4], a renowned pastor and Bible teacher, said at an elder installation I was a part of:

> *I'm going to lay my hands on these men. There is no power coming from me to these men. By laying on of hands I am ONLY identifying with these men. The only thing they can get from my hands is a disease. There is no power of any kind brought about.*

We see from what McGee said that Protestants tend to be somewhat gnostic in their faith - valuing the spiritual and devaluing the material. Catholics are not materialists but believe that God created material and became material (in fleshed -

---

[3]Water/Spirit in baptism or Bread/Wine and its consecration (the spiritual act of a Priest changing the bread and wine into the body of Christ through power given him by Jesus. No other pastors have this power. No wonder most Protestants do not subscribe to Sacraments and the full Catholic view of the Eucharist. They would have to become Catholic to receive this promised power given to the Catholic Apostles in Jesus day).

[4] Once pastor of Church Of The Open Door, Los Angeles, at the time one of the largest churches in the L.A. area. He also hosted, Through The Bible on radio for decades and is still now listened to though he died years ago. I interned at his church in 1966.

incarnate) in the person of Jesus (absolute deity and perfect humanity).

The non-material Protestants are latent gnostics because they see that matter is not important - only the spirit. Because of this, for most Protestants, the sacraments are not necessary. Thus the sacraments are emptied of their power and significance, becoming only symbolic memorials. The real, important thing is a public profession of faith - the personal trusting of Jesus Christ as Savior and Lord. That's it. Write the date in your Bible - the date you RECEIVED Christ as your personal Lord and Savior.

Now I am not saying that modern Protestants have gone as far as the ancient gnostics. But there is a similarity. Both gnostics and Protestants see salvation as occurring in the head - an individual *gnosis*. The Church is not really that important. After all, the Church is invisible (spiritual) and composed of all true believers, whoever they are. The visible Church is to be shunned. The SPIRITUAL Church is what really counts - a quasi gnostic belief.

In this True Church, the One Holy Catholic and Apostolic Church, the one Jesus organized and set into existence, includes all of our senses and is thereby a "sensual" Church because of that. It is not just a spiritual organism but an organization that involves every sense - hearing, tasting, feeling, smelling and of course seeing.

Even in the Eucharist we SEE, FEEL, TASTE, SMELL and HEAR God himself in Jesus Christ incarnated, transformed from bread and wine into his very life - his body, blood, soul and divinity. What a visual feast as we see the Priest change, through the power given him through the Apostles, the bread and wine into the body and blood of Christ. It is a miracle that happens right before our eyes! What a visual, sensual treat!

And then we consume the Living Lord - bread that becomes his body, wine that becomes his blood.

Taste and see that the Lord is good.

Go into any one of the great Catholic Cathedrals of the world and you see that our faith is surrounded by our senses - the great architecture, the art and all the beauty that lifts up our spirits. The material Church LIFTS our spirits to God - the material is a vehicle to move our souls and spirits, capturing our hearts in praise to our great God.

Though some Protestants see that something actually happens through a Sacrament - i.e. baptism bringing about regeneration, they do not value THE TRUE MATTER or material of the Eucharist, that the bread becomes true FLESH and the wine becomes true BLOOD of Christ.

David Armstrong quotes these men below in an article on the Eucharist and the Incarnation.[5]

> **The Eucharist is meant to be the continuation of the Incarnation...***As the elevating and transforming power of the Incarnation is continued and perfected in the spiritual mode of that body's existence, so t***he union of the invisible with the visible, of the divine with the human***, which we observed in the Incarnation, is distinctly brought out in its sacramental existence.*
>
> *Is not the Scripture full of incomprehensible mysteries? Do you not believe in the Trinity — a mystery not only above, but apparently contrary to reason? Do you not admit the Incarnation — that the helpless infant in Bethlehem was God? I*

---

[5] See David Armstrong, Protestant defender of the Faith who became Catholic after much study and research. He has many books worth reading, one of his first being: *A Biblical Defense of Catholicism.*

31

understand why Rationalists, who admit nothing above their reason, reject the Real Presence; but that Bible Christians should reject it is to me incomprehensible.

James Cardinal Gibbons

How, precisely, we may speak of bread and wine as Christ's Body and Blood is as baffling as how we may speak of **Jesus as both man and God**, *or of His mother as a virgin, or of the Bible as the Word of God. The matter will not yield itself either to chemistry or logic . . .*

The human mind, and perhaps especially the `spiritual' mind, has a deep-running suspicion of anything that really does bridge the gulf between spirit and matter.

Thomas Howard

Why go into all this when we are talking about the Eucharist?

You see, the Eucharist involves BOTH SPIRIT AND FLESH. To receive Jesus spiritually is a great thing. We all need to do that and keep doing that.

Yet Jesus is MORE THAN A SPIRIT. He is also FLESH. He is not just God the Spirit, but also God in a body, FLESH given for our salvation.

Why, then, receive Jesus as Spirit only? Why not receive HIM in TOTAL, Spirit and FLESH?

> By eating the Body and drinking the Blood of Christ in the Eucharist we become united to the person of Christ through his humanity. "Whoever eats my flesh and drinks my blood remains in me and I in him" (Jn 6:56). In being **united to the humanity** of Christ we are at the same time **united to his divinity**. Our mortal and corruptible natures are transformed by being joined to the source of life.[6]

Therefore I invite you to receive the TOTAL JESUS. To receive him as a symbol at communion is to short-change yourself. You get only half of Jesus. You do not get the TOTAL gift that he gave for you.

---

[6]United State Conference of Catholic Bishops
Produced by the Committee on Doctrine of the United States Conference of Catholic Bishops and approved by the full body of bishops at their June 2001 General Meeting.

In fact, many Protestants do not get Jesus at all in communion. It is only a symbol. Symbols are not the real thing.

They that worship him must worship him in Spirit and in Truth - not just in Spirit but it must be in TRUTH - all of Jesus, his Spirit and his Flesh - all of him.

So here's a question:

Have you received the TOTAL Jesus Christ as your personal Lord and Savior?

To do this, one must not only recognize their sins, invite Christ into their lives as Savior and Lord and be baptized,[7] but also receive HIS FLESH and blood in the Eucharist - the body, blood, soul and divinity of Christ.

And you can't do this in a Baptist, Presbyterian, Methodist, Bible or any other Protestant church. You receive NOTHING during communion.

---

[7]For those who believe in the power of the Sacraments, the Sacrament of Baptism - the material of water connected to the spiritual part - the Holy Spirit, "Born of WATER and SPIRIT - John 3, brings about the new birth - being "born again." Again in Titus 3:5 St. Paul talks about conversion as a WASHING of regeneration (baptism - water) and a renewing of the Holy Spirit - Spirit connecting BOTH matter (water) and spirit (Holy Spirit).

I say this not to denigrate what a typical Baptist or other denomination is doing. Realize that I was a Protestant pastor for 35 years, and communion was a reverent time of devotion to Christ. Our hearts were full of appreciation as we took the bread and drank the grape juice (many use grape juice because they are against alcoholic beverages, again going against what Jesus actually did as he used wine at the first celebration of the Eucharist).

Don't confuse a love for Christ and appreciation of his death when you receive communion to the act of actually EATING the FLESH of Christ and DRINKING his BLOOD as one receives the TOTAL CHRIST, all of him with NOTHING MISSING - all of the man, all of the God, ALL EN TOTAL!

Just because you FEEL GOOD after taking communion, just because you have that special reverence for Christ, does not mean that's all you need. You are short changing yourself if all you get is a piece of bread and some grape juice served in a small plastic cup.

Did you ever think what happens to the left over bread and grape juice? It's dumped in the trash or emptied down the drain. Why? BECAUSE THERE

IS NOTHING SPECIAL ABOUT THE ELEMENTS - the bread and grape juice that you took.

In the Catholic Church it is totally different. Because the bread and wine become the FLESH and BLOOD of Christ, they can't be thrown into the trash or poured down into the drain that is ultimately connected with the sewer. Not on your life!

What happens?

The consecrated bread goes into the Tabernacle (a place that holds Jesus) and any left over wine is consumed. If there are crumbs and residue of wine, it is sent down a special drain called the sacrarium in the sacristy that goes into the ground - never in the sewer!

So, because Catholics have great respect and reverence not only for the communion service, but for the actual elements of this service, they are treated with this TOTAL respect because it is the TOTAL JESUS.

In a Lutheran, Anglican, Episcopalian, and a few other churches, communion is a Sacrament where the PRESENCE (the spiritual presence of Jesus) is present in the bread and the wine. This kind of communion is closer, but not close enough.

The Baptists and others receive NOTHING at communion. Lutherans and others receive Jesus Spiritually, a step in the right direction.

It is only Catholics and Orthodox who receive the TOTAL JESUS - FLESH and SPIRIT.

Keep reading. It will all come into focus.

6

"THIS IS"
The Simple, Straightforward Words
Jesus Spoke

S O SIMPLE. SO POWERFUL. So open and revealing.

*THIS **IS** MY BODY*

*THIS **IS** MY BLOOD*

How can anyone miss it and distort it?

Yet the Protestant world does - almost all of them. Some of them come close but not nearly close enough.

It was the Passover night when Jesus uttered these words, "THIS IS."

To understand them more fully, we must understand the Passover and what occurred on the night of that event.

The Jews always found a lamb without blemish, this lamb that was to ultimately picture Jesus Christ who was, as St. John called: "The lamb of God who would take away the sin of the world." He also referred to Jesus in the book of Revelation saying: "I saw a lamb as if slain…and the elders saying: Worthy is the lamb that was slain to receive honor, glory and power…"

The LAMB.

That was very important in the Jewish feast of the Passover. And when you roast a lamb, it has to be consumed. Eating the sacrificial lamb was an important and essential part of the Passover celebration, and, as a result, brought about a communion of all involved - a communion with the lamb and with each other.

It is so clearly taught that the FLESH of the lamb had to be consumed after the sacrifice. This was not symbolically done! No! It is crazy to even think of it in this way.

St. Paul says:

> *Christ, our pascal lamb, has been sacrificed. Let us celebrate the festival.*
> I Cor. 5:7-8

Jesus is the lamb. And what do you do with the lamb that was slain? You eat it.

Doesn't it make sense when Jesus says in John 6,

> *Unless you eat my FLESH and drink my BLOOD you will not have my life in you?*

The lamb has to be eaten. FLESH is an essential part of the Passover as well as the Christian Communion.

This is why the Eucharist is so vital in the life of the Christian. It is in this meal where we consume Christ's FLESH and BLOOD that we experience a profound unity - he in us and we in him. It is this union that changes everything.

Yet there was no lamb on that last night with the disciples - only bread and wine. Where was the lamb if that was so important?

Listen.

There was the lamb there, right in the midst of the disciples - the LAMB, JESUS. He was the lamb that was "SLAIN BEFORE THE FOUNDATIONS OF THE WORLD" Rev. 13:8

"Lamb slain from the foundation of the world"

The Greek order of words favors this translation. He was slain in the Father's eternal counsels [8]

So at the Last Supper we see Jesus the Lamb - slain. Now, after the sacrifice of the lamb, it had to be eaten.

Was he to give them a piece of his flesh at this time?

Yes!

The bread became his flesh. The wine became his blood. They ate the FLESH of the Lamb of God and drank his blood - blood that at the first Passover was placed on the door post of each Jewish home, now, in that upper room, was applied to all who

[8]**Jamieson-Fausset-Brown Bible Commentary** *(Greek language scholars)*

drank, so that the death angel who went by the Israelite homes in Egypt would pass over them and they would find eternal life.

The disciples ATE THE LAMB, JESUS CHRIST THAT EVENING - his FLESH and BLOOD - ALL OF HIM (body, blood, soul and divinity).

And they could do it even before his actual crucifixion, because he had already been slain - before the foundations of the world. His death had already been consummated in the Father's time - a time which is not like our time.

Do you understand time? Do you understand the infinite and the way he lives WITHOUT TIME, without the constraints we have? Thus Jesus, the lamb could sit there with his disciples and offer them the Passover meal - the lamb slain for their sins.

What a picture! What an event! What a salvation - the Passover lamb there with the disciples AND THEY ATE HIM - his body, his blood.

And were changed!

WOW!

So when Jesus said: THIS IS MY BODY, THIS IS MY BLOOD, you can see how all this fits into the Passover account, and that he, the Lamb, was offering himself, the sacrificed lamb as food for their souls.[9]

And, may I say, that this is exactly what the Catholic Church does at Mass - offer the FLESH (bread) and BLOOD (wine) to all who come to receive it - receive Jesus as the LAMB OF GOD who gives his life (body, blood, soul and divinity) for the world.

One thing we must realize is that no Protestant can really have the FLESH and BLOOD of Christ unless they go to The Catholic Church. To really believe that the bread and wine become Christ's body and blood, you have to be a Catholic.

Why?

The only person who can perform this great miracle today is a Priest. And they can only do it BECAUSE THEY ARE IN THE DIRECT LINE OF

---

[9] Too many Protestants try to deflect Jesus' obvious statement by saying that he also said: "I am the door," or "I am the vine," etc. I will cover these objections later in the book.

CHRIST - directly connected to that declaration given at the Lord's Supper.

The PRIEST IS CHRIST OFFERING HIMSELF!

It is interesting that you can trace every Catholic Priest's linage to Christ as you follow who ordained him (Bishops) and who ordained them - and it will take you to the first Pope - Peter, and then to Christ.

My friends, this is not just a lot of mumbo jumbo - a lot of religious talk that means nothing. I am writing about a life and death matter, the salvation of your soul. This is TRUTH that will set your mind and soul free and bring you in touch with the TOTAL JESUS.

Later on in this book, you will read some miraculous accounts - miracles that demonstrate outwardly what is inwardly true of the Eucharist, that it is both the FLESH and SPIRIT of Christ Jesus our Lord - body, blood, souls and divinity of our Savior.

All people should be beating down the doors of our local Catholic Churches, begging our priests for the Blessed Sacrament, begging to TOUCH the TOTAL JESUS.

Oh, yes, he is omnipresent, spiritually, but ONLY PRESENT INCARNATIONALLY in the Eucharist - his physical presence in the bread and the wine.

It is here you can TOUCH Jesus, consume him and be radically changed.

You can't Skype the Mass and experience all of it. Jesus doesn't make Telehealth visits, or let us worship him in our private homes and considers that enough. No! He wants us to touch him as he wants to touch us in this Holy Sacred rite of the Eucharist.

Our corporate worship as Catholics is a must, to gain all of Jesus. It is here that we are not only united to those in the congregation surrounding us, but with the entire community of saints in heaven, all joining us in this great and holy celebration of our Savior.

7

The CLEAR TEACHING Of
John 6

S O MANY PROTESTANTS SAY:

If it's not in the Bible, I won't believe it.

Too often the issue of how to understand the Eucharist and John 6 seems to be nothing more than a hodgepodge of opinions. It appears when one reads in any depth on this subject that there is, within Protestant circles, only a wide breadth of contradictory opinions without any real sense of urgency to solve the stark, bold teaching found in John 6.

So let me make a bold statement.

The CLEAR TEACHING of eating Christ's flesh and drinking his blood is, without question, taught in John 6.   If one believes at all in following the

OBVIOUS statement of the text, they would become a Catholic and obey the clear teaching of this passage.

Let's look at the passage as a whole. I am not going to go into detail but only hit the highlights of this great chapter, a chapter filled with some awesome miracles.

1. THE FEEDING OF THE 5,000. Jesus takes bread and fish and multiplies it - a little bit that feeds a mass of people. Impossible? Yes. But Jesus loved to do the impossible, and he could because he was God in the flesh. This demonstrated Jesus' power over nature. Bread was changed - from a little to a lot. So too with the fish. The result of the crowd - SATISFACTION. And like Moses, Jesus provided bread to eat that resulted from a spectacular miracle. This was a tremendous WOW effect. Who is this one who can take so little and make it into so much!

The crowd loved Moses who gave them bread that was not from the natural realm. This manna was the bread of angels, a miracle in the making and satisfying in the eating.

So too the bread that Jesus made - not from the natural realm. A few loaves became enough to feed 5,000 plus women and children! How much bread would it take to feed that many so they were satisfied?

You would need over 500 loaves of bread (the kind you find in your grocery store) to make each person a fish sandwich. So you see the miracle. Plus all the women and children who also needed to eat! This was not a symbol that meant something else (I have heard that Jesus didn't make this much bread because he couldn't. So what really happened? With just a minute taste, just a crumb, they felt full. They say this was the miracle - nonsense!). The miracle was actual, real, and had thousands of people who would testify to this amazing event.

Later, at the last supper, Jesus did exactly the same thing. He took bread, blessed it and gave it to his disciples and told them to take it to the world. And they are still doing that today - taking the bread of life, the Eucharist, and bringing it daily to a world that is hungry for this bread from heaven.

2. JESUS WALKS ON WATER. Moses was able to help the Israelites walk *THROUGH* the water

at the Red Sea. Jesus was able to walk *ON* the water as he came to his frightened disciples. In this chapter it is vividly clear that Jesus is the Son of God who makes nature do what HE wants. It proves that he is Lord of all things as everything submits to his power and wishes - even water.

3. JESUS IS LORD OF TIME. As Jesus entered the boat, they were suddenly at the shore - another miracle! What would have taken an hour or more took only a second - bam! They were there. Who has control of time? We all are bound to it. But not Jesus. He is the Master of time. Moses was great, but here was one far greater than Moses - Jesus Christ the Mighty God.

Do you see what is happening here in John 6? This is an incredible chapter of miracle after miracle after miracle. And it is in the context of these miracles - impossible actions that Jesus accomplishes - that we see the miracle of how his body becomes FLESH to feed the world.

Impossible? How can it be?

With God…all things are possible.

You see, the Christian life is a miracle life. Too many Christians are into Churchianity - going to church, doing the things of the church but not living out the life of the True Church - the life of abiding in Christ and experiencing his life in them, the miracle of living a life impossible to live apart from the nurturing life of Jesus.

4. THE TEACHING ON THE EUCHARIST - THE FOUNDATION OF A MIRACLE THAT OCCURS AT EVERY MASS SINCE THEN. Those who were fed by Jesus and followed him asked for a sign, an obvious signal from God that he was the promised Messiah, that one greater than Moses who would come and restore the kingdom.

Jesus talks about what Moses did - the miracle manna, then he talks about what he will do - A GREATER MIRACLE. In fact, the miracle that Jesus will accomplish IS HIMSELF. He is not just going to make some manna to show his power and personhood. No. He is going to give them bread and drink that will satisfy them far beyond the manna in the desert given by Moses.

> *"Truly, truly, I say to you, it was not Moses who gave you the bread from heaven; my*

Father gives you the true bread from Heaven. For the bread of God is that which comes down from heaven, and gives life to the world...I am the Bread of life; he who comes to me shall not hunger and he who believes in me shall never thirst."

Jn 6:32-33, 35

At this point Jesus makes his great claim:

I AM the bread of life. He who comes to me will never hunger, and he who believes in me will never thirst.

What a radical statement by Jesus! And the crowd can't accept it. "How can this man top Moses? Who does he think he is," they ask?

Jesus continues building on his radical, unbelievable statements, not believed then and even now by many Christians today.

Your fathers ate the manna in the wilderness, and they died. This is the bread which comes down from heaven, that a man may eat of it and not die. I am the living bread which came down from heaven; if anyone eats of this bread, he will live for ever; and the bread which I shall give for the life of the world is my FLESH.

Jn 6:49-51

When Jesus used the word FLESH, it was shocking. He had already disturbed the crowd by saying he was the bread of life. Now he talked about giving his FLESH to the world - that bread being his very own body - (FLESH and BLOOD[10]).

Yet he doesn't stop with that. He outwardly declares that they must eat his FLESH and drink his BLOOD.

Has he gone crazy, most of the crowd thinks?

It was wonderful when he fed us REAL bread. But now he wants us to become like a cannibal and eat his FLESH? Disgusting![11]

Why were they so turned off by this teaching?

---

[10] ""When I see the BLOOD, I will pass over you." Ex. 12:13. "The BLOOD of Jesus cleanses us from all sin." I Jn. 1:9

[11] See my chapter on the Eucharist and cannibalism.

Jesus did not just convey the thought of eating his FLESH in some kind of symbolic way. No! He used a unique word for eating (*trogo* in Greek) that means to "chew" or to "gnaw." And the crowd understood exactly what he was saying. They gasped - and began to walk away. Jesus teaching on the Eucharist was too hard for them to grasp.

Even though they had experienced full bellies, eating the bread he produced from a boy's lunch, they were unwilling to come to him, to eat the eternal bread - his FLESH and find eternal life.

Yet the Apostles, those men who were to be the foundation of the Church, stay. Why? They BELIEVED in this one who was the bread of life and who would be their food that would bring eternal life.

So the question: "Do you believe? Will you accept the true, real and consumable FLESH and BLOOD of Jesus Christ?

St. Paul teaches that when we take the Eucharist we PARTICIPATE in the BLOOD of Christ in

I Corinthians 10 - an obvious indication of the reality of wine that had been transformed into Christ's holy blood.

Again, in I Corinthians 11: 27 we read:

Whoever eats the bread or drinks the cup of the Lord in an unworthy manner, will be guilty of profaning the BODY and BLOOD of the Lord.

Notice this: They are GUILTY of murder! How can this be if the body and blood are only a symbol? To be guilty of the blood of someone means you have killed them. You cannot kill a symbol - only a real person. Thus if you do not take the Eucharist in a worthy manner, you have blood on your hands, guilty of the actual crucifixion of Christ Jesus our Lord - our Passover.

Back to John 6, we see that the Apostles had seen some great miracles that day - feeding the 5,000, Jesus walking on water, Jesus getting into their boat and suddenly they were at their destination, and then the great teaching about their Master - he was the bread of life and his

FLESH would be the food that brings eternal life.

He said it. It's so clear that one would have to twist the text to say otherwise. But Protestants must deny the clear teaching of this text. Why?

Look at a coming chapter.[12]

---

[12] Real reason many Protestants do not profess the Eucharist to be the true and real FLESH and BLOOD of Christ is they have no priest. More on this in a later chapter.

8

Eating Jesus' Flesh And Cannibalism

MANY PROTESTANTS TODAY HAVE THE SAME REACTION as those disciples who heard Jesus teach about eating his flesh and drinking his and were scandalized,

> *This saying is hard, and who can hear it?*
>   Jn. 6:61.

St. John says many of Jesus' disciples stopped following Him due to Christ's straight forward teaching about the Eucharist.

What is obviously so "hard" about this saying is that it suggests cannibalism. And Jews were forbidden to drink blood.

If Catholics believe the Eucharist really is the body and blood of Christ, they then believe they are eating human flesh and drinking human blood.

On the surface its sounds disgusting, doesn't it?

It is easy to see why so many disciples of Jesus, people who were committed to him and his message, walked away.

Jesus was preaching heresy!

Or was he?

We are going to look below the surface, still take Jesus literally, and see whether Catholics practice a kind of spiritual cannibalism.

Not only did the Jews think Jesus was teaching cannibalism, but so did the Romans - a charge that continues to this day.

But while Holy Communion does involve eating human flesh and drinking human blood, it is not true that it is cannibalistic. How so?

1. **The Eucharist involves eating and drinking what is LIVING not what is dead.** Cannibals

kill a person and eat their dead body. By contrast, Jesus is alive. He rose again, and it is this LIVE JESUS that is in the Eucharist. We eat the FLESH and drink the BLOOD of a living person!

Amazing, isn't it!

2. **The Eucharist involves eating the WHOLE body and ALL the blood of Christ.** A cannibal only eats part of the dead body - not the whole thing including bones, etc. We, on the other hand, don't get just a piece of Jesus. We get all of him in total. When you take the consecrated Host, it seems so small - but in fact when you receive it you receive ALL OF JESUS, the infinite LORD, all enshrined in what you receive. Thus we get the TOTAL JESUS - all of him. Even if all you receive is the Host - the body, the flesh of Christ you also receive his blood since the body contains ALL OF CHRIST.

A Catholic does not have to drink from the cup to receive the blood of Christ. That blood is also included in the host and in eating it, one gets all of Christ - body, blood, soul and divinity.

3. **The Eucharist involved eating the glorified body and blood of Christ.** Jesus' body is not a resuscitated corpse like Lazarus. Instead his resurrected body was transformed into a spiritual body. So when a Catholic receives communion, he receives not just flesh, but glorified flesh, resurrected, transfigured and glorified in a super, unique body. Cannibals do not practice this in any way.

4. **The Eucharist contains the SOUL of Jesus.** Some cannibals eat the flesh of their dead victim and drink their blood in hopes of gaining the strength or personality of that person. The Christian eats the FLESH and drinks his BLOOD because Jesus is ALIVE and the Christian's immortal soul is united to Christ's body and blood. The Eucharist CANNOT BE SEPARATED from this living, breathing soul of Christ.

5. **The Eucharist contains the divinity of Jesus**. You see, Jesus is both true and perfect humanity and also absolute divinity. They are inseparable. So, as I have said before, when you take the Eucharist you receive ALL OF JESUS - IN TOTAL (body, blood, soul and divinity). The cannibal thinks he is getting

closer to God, but is, in fact, acting like a beast. When a Christian consumes the Eucharist, it, in fact consumes him as he becomes part of the body of Christ - we in him and he in us. The cannibal becomes a beast. The Christian becomes a new person - what blessing!

6. **The Eucharist is a non-violent act where a cannibal is involved in a violent crime.** The Eucharist is a non-bloody re-presentation of the sacrifice of the cross brought into the present. Jesus is NOT crucified again - that only happened once. It is that sacrifice that is brought into the present and celebrated.

So we see that the disciples who were scandalized by Jesus statement about his flesh and blood were right to be horrified. How could their great teacher be saying such absurd and repulsive things? They did not understand how humankind can find UNION with the eternal God - through this simple yet profound sacrament, the Eucharist where Jesus gives us his body and blood so that we might be saved.

In it we consume HIM and he consumes US - to the eternal glory of his name...amen!

9

"Bone of my bones, flesh of my flesh"
The First and Second Adam
TOTAL UNION

The TOTAL JESUS. That's the whole theme of this book - its central thesis. When you receive the TOTAL JESUS you then, as a glorious result, receive TOTAL UNION with Christ Jesus the Lord. Receiving Christ spiritually i.e. inviting him into your life as your Lord and Savior doesn't go far enough if you want to experience TOTAL UNION.

Protestants don't have this. They fall short because they have never received the TOTAL JESUS - all of him, his body, blood, soul and divinity.

Now this is not saying that they are not saved or that they won't go to heaven. Nor am I saying that they do not have a very close, intimate relationship with Jesus. Many Protestants do. As a Protestant pastor for 35 years, I had this kind of intimate, one-on-one relationship. So I am not concluding Protestants fall short on the relational level. They do get Jesus as their Savior when they confess their sins and receive Christ (and are baptized).[13] They can have intimacy through prayer, Scripture and that inward working of the Holy Spirit. But even with all of this…they get only half of him…

Half the person.
Half the divinity.
Half the union.

HALF!

That's tragic, isn't it?

Their subtle gnostic beliefs have kept them from the MAN, Jesus Christ - his FLESH and BLOOD. They, with great privilege, were invited into a relationship with God the Spirit, the Holy Spirit and Jesus the Spirit, but not Jesus the man - that perfect humanity that is available for us to be connected to in the Catholic Eucharist.

---

[13] I keep adding baptism because many Protestants do not believe that baptism saves. It is only an ordinance that should be practiced, but it has no eternal power to save.

Most Protestants refuse to acknowledge that the Eucharist is anything more than a symbol (or at best Christ is spiritually present in the elements).

Because they too often ridicule and act with disgust with those who do receive him, all of him in TOTAL, they miss out on the blessing of receiving ALL OF JESUS.

When Adam received his new wife, he declared:

This one—at last!—is bone from my bones, flesh from my flesh.
Gen. 2

FLESH.

It's important in an intimate relationship.

God said:

The two will become ONE FLESH.
Gen. 2

How do we become ONE FLESH with the new Adam, Jesus - the God/Man? How do we become truly ONE with him?

Marriage consists of two becoming one. It is consummated by the act of ONE FLESH - thus the two become one. So too with our UNION WITH

CHRIST - this Holy Marriage of Christ to his Bride. It is not just a spiritual act but one of FLESH - the uniting of ALL OF US - body, blood, soul with his divinity.

"She is bone of my bone, flesh of my flesh." Adam.

This is a mystery, but I am talking about Christ and his Church.

St. Paul in Ephesians 5

Here in Ephesians, St. Paul states that the "two become one flesh." In saying this, St. Paul states that he is talking about Christ and his bride, the Church.

How does this "one flesh" happen? We come back to John 6 where when we eat the FLESH of Jesus he becomes part of us and we of him - ONE FLESH.

"Bone of my bone, flesh of my flesh."

This is the language of marital intimacy.

Thus when, as a Catholic, you come to receive the bread, this is not just part of the Mass. It is a time of the most intimate of intimate moments with

Jesus - two becoming one. What ecstasy! What glory! What union!

Are you beginning to see the depth of this teaching of the Eucharist - our flesh and the FLESH of Christ becoming one - this vital union that changes us totally?

Pope Saint John Paul II often spoke about the nuptial character of the Eucharist and the sacrament of marriage.

> *The Eucharist is the sacrament of our redemption. It is the sacrament of the Bridegroom and of the Bride." Moreover, "the entire Christian life bears the mark of the spousal love of Christ and the Church. Already Baptism, the entry into the People of God, is a nuptial mystery; it is so to speak the nuptial bath which precedes the wedding feast, the Eucharist.*

Many have taken the Song of Songs to picture this deep, intimate relationship with Jesus - so deep that it can only be illustrated on the human level by a marriage that is consummated, where both the bride and the groom emerged in love - becoming one flesh. This intimacy we have with Jesus is so great that it embraces all of our senses - drinking in love, contemplating this divine encounter - flesh and FLESH producing fruit, more fruit and much fruit.[14]

So we see God's ultimate purpose for us - UNION - that glorious union, the marriage of his Son, the Groom to us his bride consummated in the reception of the Eucharist - a holy, intimate moment where two fleshes become one - to the glory of his name. Amen!

---

[14] See John 15 and the results of abiding in Christ, the vine.

10

The Eucharist Is The Only TOTAL Presence Of Jesus Today

VATICAN II STATED THAT THE EUCHARIST is the "source and summit of the Christian Life" (Lumen Gentium, 11). What does this mean? It is a declaration that ALL OTHER SACRAMENTS lead us to the Eucharist. This is the focal point of all our lives - Jesus in the Eucharist.

Vatican II is simply a statement that THERE IS NOT A MORE REAL PRESENCE OF JESUS CHRIST in the world today than what you find in the Eucharist.

Stop and think about this for a moment. Let the above sentence sink into your mind. It is something you need to process.

Until Jesus comes and this age is consummated, the Eucharist is the place where we find Jesus, the

TOTAL CHRIST, in the bread and wine. Here we see Christ PHYSICALLY and SPIRITUALLY (The God Man).

One day we will not need the Eucharist. We will, instead, have the glorified presence of Jesus in living color, in a majesty and power that our glorified bodies will be able to grasp as we fall down to worship him.

But until then, the Eucharist is the best we have, this special gift that we can see, touch, taste and receive. It is not just a visual reminder, a sign, or some kind of extra that is added to our worship. It is the CENTER of our worship, a center that impacts all that we are - body and soul, as Jesus gives us his flesh and spirit for us.

The Eucharist is not a bread God but God. It is not Jesus hiding out in the bread, but Jesus - all of him, the TOTAL JESUS there for us in full view, giving us life and strength to live each day.

During the Covid 19 crisis, many Catholics could not participate in the Mass - seeing the TOTAL Christ and receiving him, all of him in the Eucharist. In so doing they missed out on this special presence, this gift that the Catholic Church offers to people of faith.

Many Protestants do not understand this. It is foreign to their thinking and experience. They go to church to fellowship, sing, and hopefully hear a good sermon. This is not true of Catholics. We go to Mass to RECEIVE THE LIVING, EMBODIMENT OF JESUS. Jesus and his presence mean everything to us. And we find it IN THE EUCHARIST.

Protestant Evangelicals talk a lot about receiving Jesus as one's own personal Lord and Savior. That's good and even necessary. Yet they fall short because they do not receive Jesus fully, TOTALLY, all of him - Flesh and Spirit.

Catholics are honored to do this. It is a special grace to be a Catholic. We don't deserve any more grace than any other person. Yet, because of the Eucharist, because we believe what Jesus said and the Church has taught for 2,000 years, we receive this special elevated grace, the Eucharist - Christ TOTALLY present to us, with us and in us.

To HIM be the glory! Amen.

11

The Witness Of Early Church Fathers

S O YOU STILL HOLD TO YOUR INTERPRETATION of the Eucharist thinking that you have just as much right to your views as to any other view.

The Real Presence was upheld by early Christians.

It was upheld by **St. Ignatius of Antioch** in the first century:

> *Consider how contrary to the mind of God are the heterodox in regard to the grace of God which has come to us . . . They abstain from the Eucharist and from prayer, because they do not admit that the Eucharist is the flesh of our Savior Jesus Christ, the flesh which suffered for our sins and which the*

Father, in His graciousness, raised from the dead.

St. Ignatius of Antioch, *Letter to the Smyrnaeans*, circa 90 AD

It was upheld by **St. Justin Martyr** in the second century:

This food we call the Eucharist, of which no one is allowed to partake except one who believes that the things we teach are true, and has received the washing for forgiveness of sins and for rebirth, and who lives as Christ handed down to us.

For we do not receive these things as common bread or common drink; but as Jesus Christ our Savior being incarnate by God's Word took flesh and blood for our salvation, so also we have been taught that the food consecrated by the Word of prayer which comes from him, from which our flesh and blood are nourished by transformation, is the flesh and blood of that incarnate Jesus.

St. Justin Martyr, *First Apology*, circa 150 AD

It was upheld by **St. Clement of Alexandria** in the third century:

> *The one, the Watered Wine, nourishes in faith, while the other, the Spirit, leads us on to immortality. The union of both, however, – of the drink and of the Word, – is called the Eucharist, a praiseworthy and excellent gift.*
>
> *Those who partake of it in faith are sanctified in body and in soul. By the will of the Father, the divine mixture, man, is mystically united to the Spirit and to the Word.*

St. Clement of Alexandria, *The Instructor of the Children*, circa 202 AD).

It was upheld by **St. Cyril of Jerusalem** in the fourth century:

> *Since then He Himself has declared and said of the Bread, (This is My Body), who shall dare to doubt any longer? And since He has affirmed and said, (This is My Blood), who shall ever hesitate, saying, that it is not His blood?*

Do not, therefore, regard the bread and wine as simply that; for they are, according to the Master's declaration, the body and blood of Christ. Even though the senses suggest to you the other, let faith make you firm.

Do not judge in this matter by taste, but be fully assured by the faith, not doubting that you have been deemed worthy of the body and blood of Christ...[Since you are] fully convinced that the apparent bread is not bread, even though it is sensible to the taste, but the body of Christ, and that the apparent wine is not wine, even though the taste would have it so,...partake of that bread as something spiritual, and put a cheerful face on your soul.

St. Cyril of Jerusalem, *Catechetical Lectures*, circa 350 AD

St. John Chrysostom also upheld the doctrine in the fourth century

I wish to add something that is plainly awe-inspiring, but do not be astonished or upset. This Sacrifice, no matter who offers it, be it Peter or Paul, is always the same as that

which Christ gave His disciples and which priests now offer: The offering of today is in no way inferior to that which Christ offered, because it is not men who sanctify the offering of today; it is the same Christ who sanctified His own.

For just as the words which God spoke are the very same as those which the priest now speaks, so too the oblation is the very same.

St. John Chrysostom, *Homilies on the Second Epistle to Timothy*, circa 397 AD

St. Ambrose of Milan also upheld it in the fourth century:

Thus, every soul which receives the bread which comes down from heaven is a house of bread, the bread of Christ, being nourished and having its heart strengthened by the support of the heavenly bread which dwells within it.

St. Ambrose of Milan, *Letter to Horontianus*, circa 387 AD).

St. Jerome was also among the Church Fathers who upheld it:

> After the type[15] had been fulfilled by the Passover celebration and He had eaten the flesh of the lamb with His Apostles, He takes bread which strengthens the heart of man, and goes on to the true Sacrament of the Passover, so that just as Melchizedek, the priest of the Most High God, in prefiguring Him, made bread and wine an offering, He too makes Himself manifest in the reality of His own Body and Blood.
>
> St. Jerome, *Commentaries on the Gospel of Matthew*, 398 AD

St. Augustine of Hippo was also among them:

> You ought to know what you have received, what you are going to receive, and what you ought to receive daily. That Bread which you see on the altar, having been sanctified by the word of God, is the Body of Christ. The chalice, or rather, what is in that chalice,

---

15 Types are pictures, object-lessons, by which God taught His people concerning His grace and saving power.

having been sanctified by the word of God, is the Blood of Christ.

St. Augustine of Hippo, *Sermons*, circa 400 AD

And then from a unified council of the Church -

Council of Ephesus

We will necessarily add this also. Proclaiming the death, according to the flesh, of the only-begotten Son of God, that is Jesus Christ, confessing his resurrection from the dead, and his ascension into heaven, we offer the un-bloody sacrifice in the churches, and so go on to the mystical thanksgivings, and are sanctified, having received his holy flesh and the precious blood of Christ the Savior of us all.

And not as common flesh do we receive it; God forbid: nor as of a man sanctified and associated with the Word according to the unity of worth, or as having a divine indwelling, but as truly the life-giving and very flesh of the Word himself. For he is the life according to his nature as God, and when he became united to his flesh, he made it also to be life-giving.

Session 1, *Letter of Cyril to Nestorius* [A.D. 431]

If the REAL PRESENCE of Christ was taught by the early Church - those closest to the Apostles, men who KNEW the truth, why argue about it? Why not embrace this great truth delivered to us by the Holy Spirit whom Jesus promised would GUIDE US INTO ALL TRUTH?

You can see that from the earliest days of the Church, the Church fathers proclaimed UNANIMOUSLY that the Eucharist was the very BODY and BLOOD of Christ.

Even though they sometimes talked about symbol and figure, they never denied the fact that after the priest consecrated the Host and the Wine, that it became (was transubstantiated) into the body and blood of Christ (his actual FLESH and BLOOD. There was no doubt about that - never a disagreement as to this essential act and sacrament in the Catholic Church which began at the initiation of Jesus Christ.

If you are a Protestant, when did your church begin? Was it initiated by Jesus Christ himself breathing on the leaders so that they would be infused with the Holy Spirit and lead the Church into the TRUTH?

Quit fighting what is true. If Protestant, your practice of celebrating the Lord's Table is not in line with what is true. Admit it. And come eat and drink of what is true food indeed!

12

Who Has The Right To Interpret Scripture?

WHO IS RIGHT TO INTERPRET JOHN 6 or any other passage regarding the Eucharist? Is the Baptist view correct, or the Presbyterian? How about the Anglican's or the Lutheran's? Who has the AUTHORITY to interpret the Holy Scriptures and any point much less the view on the Eucharist?

Don't brush this question off as if you think that it is simple to answer.

If the Holy Spirit gave us the Holy and inspired Scriptures, wouldn't this same Holy Spirit make sure that we interpret it properly? Of course! Unity is critical in the Body of Christ.

Yet this unity has been fractured in thousands of pieces with over 40-50,000 separate groups each vying for the spot of being the true interpreters of the Word of God.

That's nonsense!

Because of this, some dip, some immerse, others pour when it comes to Baptism. Others say it is only a symbol while others, both Protestant and Catholic say it is essential, that something actually happens when one is placed in the waters of baptism - a Holy Sacrament and not just a symbol.

On and on the church is divided, not just on some minor issues, but major - salvation issues like baptism, the Eucharist and Reconciliation (confession of sins to a Priest who stands in the place of Jesus Christ the Great Hight Priest). Oh, and there are so many other things that various churches fight over and condemn each other because THEY UNDERSTAND AND PROCLAIM THE TRUTH.

How do they know?

Did Jesus give the Baptists authority to do this? What about the Presbyterians (various Presbyterian groups who broke away from each other due to deep disagreements), Lutherans (many kinds of Lutherans who can't get along) Pentecostals, Church of Christ, Disciples of Christ churches (where the Church of Christ split), Methodists who are now splitting into two groups due to various interpretations about gay life and other practices?

On and on and on and on and on. Even after Jesus in his high priestly prayer prayed fervently for the UNITY of the body of Christ -

That they might be ONE.

ONE!

Yes. That is the hope and dream of the cornerstone of the Church - Jesus Christ our Lord and Master.

Yet today there is not this unity.

And, even as you read this book, you might mock what I say, thinking I am a simpleton, old fashioned in my thinking, a belief that the Church could really be one...

ONE IN SPIRIT

ONE IN DOCTRINE
ONE IN DOGMA

ONE!

So the question is simple. How do we get this kind of unity, this ONENESS?

It was the first leader of the Church, Peter, who said:

No Scripture is of any private interpretation.

II Peter 1

If this is true, that means that the Holy Spirit who gave the Scripture will NOT reveal the truth to ME apart from the interpretation of the Church no matter how committed I am to my Faith.

You see, it is the CHURCH that was given the responsibility to interpret the Scripture. Jesus gave the apostles the AUTHORITY to do this. He didn't give it to me, or the Baptists (my dad was a very committed Baptist minister and an awesome follower of Jesus - yet, even he did not have this authority). He didn't give it to leaders of the

Methodists (no matter how great their founder was - John Wesley), or to ANY OTHER GROUP.

NO ONE HAS THE GOD GIVEN AUTHORITY TO INTERPRET THE HOLY. SCRIPTURES BUT THE CATHOLIC CHURCH - the Bishops united with the Holy Father under the promised leadership of the Holy Spirit.

> *...you should know how to behave in the household of God, which is the **CHURCH** of the living God, the PILLAR and FOUNDATION of **TRUTH**.*
>
> I Tim 3:15

Look how clear this passage is, confirming that Jesus will guide this Apostolic community of Bishops by his Holy Spirit - this special guide to keep the Bishops on track.

It is this authority that creates unity - this oneness Jesus prayed for. Without it we argue about baptism, the Sacraments, as well as what this book is about...the Eucharist.

Any other argument against the Eucharist being the true Flesh and Blood of Christ is chaff[16] - human reasoning that may make sense but is in error. You may be able to "prove" you are right through your system of interpretation, use of the languages, etc, but it is all sincere human reasoning devoid of the Spirit - a reverence to the truth gone astray.

Sincerity is good. But being absolutely in line with the truth is far better.

You cannot go against God's given authority and find truth no matter what kind of godly scholar you are. You will be a heretic.

And who wants to be that!

So, if you do what St. Peter states in II Peter 1, and privatize your interpretation of the Bible, how will you arrive at a true, Holy Spirit inspired interpretation?

We all know what the Holy Scriptures say. The real question is: What do they mean?

Interpretation is critical.

---

[16] The seed coverings and other debris separated from the seed in threshing grain - something that is basically worthless.

To find out, go to the Church that Christ established, a Church that guarantees that what it (the Bishops in union with the Bishop of Rome) says is directly from the guidance from the Holy Spirit.

Jesus said to the Apostolic community:

He (the Holy Spirit) will guide you into ALL truth.

It seems that that settles it. Take all the Baptists, Presbyterians, Methodists, Lutherans, Pentecostals, Anglicans, etc. all fighting over THEIR interpretation and submit to the Holy Spirit's interpretation of what is true through the Church Jesus set in place, The One Holy Catholic and Apostolic Church.

This Church is still in existence - just down the street from you. And for 2,000 years they have been true to the Truth - the Holy Spirit guiding them through many issues - the Trinity, is Jesus both fully God and fully man, baptism, and hundreds of issues.

This same, Holy Spirit Church has not caved in to the social and theological pressures to change with the winds of time. Most of the mainline Protestant denominations have done that - going against CLEAR teaching in the Holy Scriptures and the Holy Spirit guided teachings of the Church.

The Catholic Church has not capitulated one bit. They have held against the tidal waves of moral change and theological revision. How could they change when Jesus promised that the Holy Spirit would guide them into ALL TRUTH - including the truth of the Eucharist, that the bread and wine become the body and blood of Jesus Christ our Lord?

NEVER!

As a Protestant pastor for 35 years, I believed the Bible to be authoritative. And I was right. Every word written is the inspired word of God. But I was wrong thinking that I - me with all my study at Dallas Theological Seminary, all my work on the original languages, all my understanding of hermeneutics (the study of interpretation) would lead me to the truth.

I was sincere as I read other divergent opinions and interpretations on a passage I was studying. And I believed the Holy Spirit was guiding me. But what

about that other sincere Protestant Evangelical pastor who took issue with my interpretation?
WHO WAS RIGHT?

I wanted to preach what was truth - true TRUTH.

I had the Bible - but I wasn't given the Holy Spirit's interpretation of those words - words which have fragmented so many Protestants today.

It wasn't until I became Catholic that all was settled. I knew I could stake my life on what Jesus said to those early apostles - the Holy Spirit would guide them (and their successors[17]) into all truth.

AUTHORITY.

Can you trust the Holy Spirit to speak the truth all the time? If you believe that he can, you have no choice but to become Catholic and embrace the TRUTH she professes, guided by the Holy Spirit.

---

[17] Read David Armstrong on this issue or other Catholic apologists

13

The REAL Reason Why Most Protestants Do Not Take John 6 Literally

I WAS A PROTESTANT EVANGELICAL PASTOR FOR 35 YEARS and helped grow one of the largest churches in the Dallas Ft. Worth area. We had communion once a month. And though it was tacked on to our typical Sunday morning worship service, we did it reverently as an expression of our deepest gratitude for Christ and his sacrifice for our sins.

There were even some times when we would set aside a whole service just to focus on the Eucharist and what it meant for all of us who believe.

It was an awesome event.
So this book is not at all a denial of the meaning of communion for all of the Christian community, whether Catholic, Orthodox or Protestant. There is

in all these groups the central focus of what it means for Jesus to die for us and bring us eternal life though that gift.

Then why should I be so brash to say that Protestants get only half of Jesus?

I say this because it is true, it's what the Bible clearly teaches, and not only that, but the history of the Church clear back to the beginning screams out these facts - The Eucharist is NOT just a symbol, but, when celebrated by a Priest, becomes the actual, living, breathing, soul-filled FLESH AND BLOOD of Christ Jesus our Lord.

Though one can try to refute this, they are on thin ice. They must deny the clear teaching of the Scriptures as well as what the early Church taught through its leadership.

Now pay close attention to this reason why most Protestants will not take John 6 literally. It's subtle, but it is there, nevertheless.

THEY DON'T HAVE ANY PRIESTS.

Protestants have only pastors who are ordained but NOT GIVEN THE POWER BY CHRIST TO, WITH

CHRIST'S POWER, TRANSFORM THE BREAD AND WINE INTO THE BODY (FLESH) AND WINE (BLOOD) OF CHRIST.

There can be no Eucharist without the priesthood, just as there can be no priesthood without the Eucharist.

St. John Paul II

That's it.

NO PRIEST, NO EUCHARIST

Or even take it further…

No priest, no Eucharist, no Church!

Now I said it.

I have stated a truth that MUST BE DEALT WITH by Protestants.

They MUST come up with another interpretation for John 6, change it into a symbol and make Jesus FLESH and BLOOD only a symbol of belief.

Are they right about believing Jesus?

YES!

But they are wrong about the intent of what Jesus said. All of Church history screams this out.

So Martin Luther, Calvin and the others realized that the central focus of the Church had to change. Many churches put the podium in the center - the preaching of the Word of God. It is good to preach the Word, but sad they took out the Altar, and in many cases removed it. Why?

No pastor could do what ONLY A PRIEST COULD DO.. So they got rid of the Altar.

Sad, isn't it?

They would rather practice their newly founded religion than submit to the truth - Jesus gave his FLESH AND BLOOD for us and wants to give that same FLESH AND BLOOD that was slain to us!

What truth!

Yet the Protestant leaders distorted, came close, but could never carry out a true Mass - the commemoration of the death of Jesus for our sins through EATING his FLESH and DRINKING his BLOOD.

Thousands of Catholic Churches during the early Protestant Reformation had bands of Protestant armies who went through and cleansed Catholic churches, tearing out the Tabernacle (that held the TRUE FLESH of Jesus) and destroying the Altars.

In so doing they ripped up the true words of Jesus in John 6, tearing them out of context and making them say what they did not say.

All to CONTROL THE PEOPLE.

They wanted PROTESTANT POWER. So they ripped out the HEART of the Church - the very sustaining life of the Church - JESUS CHRIST.

How sad, isn't it, that they destroyed the central teaching of the Church through the ages.

The STARK REALITY is this: If I were a pastor of a Protestant church and changed my beliefs on the Eucharist, adopting what the Catholics taught, I would have to resign.

Protestant pastors HAVE NO AUTHORITY OR DIVINE POWER to celebrate the Eucharist. I could no longer conduct communion that was a heretical action going against the clear and concise teaching of Jesus Christ and the Church he established.

Not many pastors are willing to resign. So they go on and on and on, kidding themselves that what they do is backed up by Jesus, when, in fact, it's a lie.

I know that these are very strong words, words issued to many pastors I love and honor for the many things they do as they lead their churches.

I was one of them. And then...I had to resign. It cost me nearly $1,000,000 to do so. All my training was as a pastor and Evangelical leader. And, since I was nearly 60 years old, I could never get the kind of salary nearly to what I was making when I headed up Community Bible Study International (CBSI).

Yet I never was sad that I did. I had to follow the truth no matter what the cost.

There are times that the sole reason Protestant pastors will not become Catholic is ECONOMIC -

money. And I do not say this lightly. I know the pressures to keep my job so that I could provide for my family.

WHY PROTESTANT PASTORS WILL NOT BECOME CATHOLIC

1. **FAITH** - DON'T BELIEVE
2. **ECONOMIC** - LOSE MONEY
3. **PRESTIGE** - LOSS OF RESPECT

One of the great tragedies of the Reformation is the loss of authentic Holy Orders - legitimate ordination in Protestant churches. The loss of that meant the LOSS OF THE REAL PRESENCE IN HOLY COMMUNION, and no true ordination into the Priesthood means no true communion, only a memory of what was, not a bringing into the present of what is - the BODY and BLOOD of Jesus Christ our Savior.

Because of this tragedy, Protestant pastors cannot properly consecrate the elements, and therefore transubstantiation cannot occur. All Protestants have is bread and wine (or grape juice). That's it! There is no miracle that occurs on the altar. Just the matter, bread and wine, devoid of the SPIRIT.

NOTHING HAPPENS!

How tragic!

What emptiness when Protestants could have more - more than just bread and wine, MORE OF JESUS! All of him. THE TOTAL JESUS!

This is not to say that the sincerity of their actions are well intended. As I have stated before, they do remember Jesus and his sacrifice for sins. That is good. But they, because there is not vested authority to change bread in the BODY and wine into the BLOOD of Christ, fall far short.

This is a grievous tragedy beyond what one can imagine. And countless millions of Protestants go hungry for the TRUE bread of life - Jesus Christ who gives this life, his flesh and blood, at every Mass in the Catholic Church.

Millions have been denied real food that brings eternal life.

LORD.

Bring us all together into that

One Holy Catholic and Apostolic Church

that we might be one

and enjoy the fruit of that unity,

a fellowship in your

BODY and BLOOD

and as a result

experience your full and

TOTAL Life.

Amen

14

Miracles That Prove The Eucharist Is Truly Flesh and Blood

W HEN I WRITE ABOUT MIRACLES, I mean just that. These miracles I will offer you are not just rumors or stories told that got twisted or exaggerated. The Catholic Church doesn't do that.

As Christians, we do recognize miracles, events that happen that can't be explained unless there is divine intervention. The turning a boys lunch into a meal that fed over 5,000 - a miracle. Jesus walking on water, all the healings of the blind, the lepers, and even those raised from the dead - like Lazarus - miracles. Of course there is the resurrection and ascension as well as all the miracles performed by the apostles. All can't be explained in any other way. They really happened and confirm for us all the reality of the supernatural and reassure us of God's greatness.

But the Catholic Church will not believe everything that is difficult to explain as a miracle. There are strict procedures and examinations of each so called miracle to ensure that is is truly of supernatural origin.

The Church must have HARD EVIDENCE to say that an event or happening is a miracle.

For example, one of the most common types of miracles is a sudden healing of a person. For this cure to be considered a miracle, the disease must be of a serious nature as to be impossible to cure by a doctor or through medicine.

For a miracle of healing to occur it must be spontaneous, complete and permanent. To ensure that this is the case, the local Bishop has the authority to investigate, create a board of medical professionals to evaluate the event who then report the results.

In most cases, what some call a miracle cannot be confirmed to be that, even though God may have intervened as he used medicine, a doctor, or time to bring healing.

For example, in Lourdes, the Medical Commission documented over 8,000 extraordinary cures but validated only 70 of them as true miracles.

I say all of this to emphasize that the Church has a healthy skepticism when it comes to a miracle. Whether it be an apparition of the Blessed Mother or a Eucharistic miracle, it is ALWAYS INVESTIGATED.

But with all of the skepticism of the Church, miracles are proclaimed and proven on a regular basis. Why? God still loves to show his loving power to do what seems impossible!

So with this in mind, let me share with you some miracles about the Eucharist - miracles which have been verified through intense scrutiny and disciplined study.

Yet in one sense, WHY DO I EVEN HAVE TO SHOW VISIBLE SIGNS that the bread is the body and the wine becomes blood.

I have talked to people who WANT PROOF that the bread and wine are TRANSFORMED into the FLESH and BLOOD of Christ our Lord.

PROOF! Really?

You don't need proof that when you became a Christian YOU BECAME A BRAND NEW PERSON ON THE INSIDE - totally changed, transformed into a NEW CREATURE as you were placed in the waters baptism (or as some Evangelicals say, "put your faith in Christ as Savior and Lord").

There is no proof. You weigh the same, look the same, and have the same personality. On the outside, all is the same. Yet, BY FAITH, you were born again and became a child of God.

WHAT A CHANGE!

Incredible! A miracle of God's grace!

Yet the same people who fight against any change in the elements of communion, fight because it seems ridiculous. The elements appear to be the same. But, by the power of the Holy Spirit, and the authority of Jesus Christ working through the priest,

ALL IS CHANGED, just as you were through the waters of baptism.

And, much like all of the Christian life, it takes FAITH.

So, I will offer some miracles that are verified. Yet in the end, it will take your faith ignited by the Holy Spirit.

1. Bloodstained Cloths

In 1263, A German priest, Peter of Prague, had doubts about the doctrine of transubstantiation - the bread and wine being transformed into the body and blood, soul and divinity of Christ. As this priest began to celebrate the Mass in Bolseno, Italy, and consecrated the bread and wine, blood began to stream out of the Host onto the altar linen (corporal).

This was reported to Pope Urban IV who, after a through investigation, concluded it was a miracle.

The blood stained linen is still exhibited at the Cathedral in Orvieto, Italy. Many miracles have occurred where the Host turns into the flesh and blood of Christ.

2. Dropped Host Turns Cloth Bloody

It was at Mass on Easter Sunday, 1331, in Blanot which is a small village in the central part of France that communion was given to a Jacquette. The priest placed the host on her tongue and walked away. Yet the Host fell from her mouth to a cloth she was holding. But the time the priest saw what happened, he went back to receive the fallen Host. What he saw surprised him - a spot of blood on the cloth where the Host fell.

After the Mass, the priest took the cloth to the sacristy and began to wash it, but the more he washed the larger the spot of blood became ultimately growing to the size of a sacred Host. He took the cloth and cut out that piece that was blooded and placed it in the tabernacle with the other Hosts. Those Hosts were never distributed but remained perfectly preserved for hundreds of years.

The bloodstained cloth has been preserved in St. Martin's Church in Blanot and is brought out every feast of Corpus Christi.

3. A Bright Light Emitted

It was 1247 when a woman in Santare, Portugal, was concerned about her husband's faithfulness. So she went to a sorceress who promised the woman that her husband would go back to his loving ways if she would bring a consecrated Host back to her.

The woman agreed.

The next Mass, the woman put a consecrated Host in her handkerchief. Yet before she could return it to the sorceress, the handkerchief became-stained with blood. You can imagine how frightened the woman was. She hurried home and hid the blood stained handkerchief in a bedroom drawer.

But that wasn't the end of this miracle.

That night a bright light emitted from that bedroom drawer. When her husband saw it, the woman told him the entire story.

The following day many came from the town to see this bright light.

Finally, it was reported to a parish priest who, after going to the house, took the blood stained handkerchief to his Church and put it in a wax container where it continued to bleed for three days.

After the Host stayed in the wax container for four years, the priest opened the tabernacle door and saw that the wax container had broken into numerous pieces. In its place was a crystal container with the blood inside. And now on the second Sunday of April, the incident is re-enacted in the Church of St. Stephen in Santarem. And the reliquary that houses the miraculous Host stands above the tabernacle in that Church.

4. Monstrance Stolen Containing Consecrated Hosts

In the village of Wale, near Krakow, Poland, thieves broke into the Church and stole the monstrance containing consecrated Hosts. After they discovered the monstrance was not made of gold, they threw it into marshlands nearby.

After it grew dark, a light emanated from the place where the monstrance and consecrated Hosts had been dumped. This light was visible for several kilometers, and villagers became afraid and reported what was happening to the bishop of Krakow.

The bishop ordered that there be three days of fasting and prayer after which he found the monstrance and consecrated Hosts which were found unbroken.

Every year now, during the feast of the Corpus Christi, this miracle is celebrated in Corpus Christi Church in Krokow.

5. The Face of the Christ Child

On June 2, 1649, in Eten, Peru, Father Jerome Silva was ready to replace the monstrance in the tabernacle when he saw in the Host the image of a child with thick brown curls falling to his shoulders. He showed the Host to those present, and they all agreed that the image of a child was Jesus Christ.

The next month, during the exhibition of the Eucharist, the Child Jesus appeared in the Host again. He was dressed in a purple habit in a way that was the custom of the local Indians, the Mochicas. The apparition lasted for fifteen minutes with many people witnessing this event, with three small hearts (symbolizing the Trinity) also visible.

This is celebrated by thousands each year.

6. Three Dots Of Blood

On April, 28, 2001 in Trivandrum, India Father Johnson Karoor was saying Mass when he saw three dots of blood on the consecrated Host. At that he stopped reciting the prayers and spent some time staring at the Eucharist. He then asked those at Mass to look at what he saw. Then he asked the faithful to remain in prayer in this verified miracle.

7. Water Of A Flood Held At Bay

In Avignon, France, November 1433, a small Church operated by the Gray Penitents of the Franciscan order was exhibiting a consecrated Host for perpetual adoration. After several days of heavy rain, the local rivers (Sorgue and One) began to flood the town.

The head of the order took a boat to the Church knowing that it had been destroyed. But instead, those in the boat saw a miracle. Although the waters were four feet high around the Church, the pathway from the doorway to the altar was absolutely dry and the sacred Host was untouched by the raging waters - like what happened when the Children of Israel walked across the Red Sea on dry land.

Amazed by this miracle, they invited the Friars to verify the miracle along with many townspeople and authorities who came to the Church singing praise and thanks to the Lord.

Today, the Gray Penitent brothers reunite at the Chapelle des Penitents Gris every November 30 to celebrate this awesome miracle.

8. Basilian Monk Doubts The Real Presence

In the city of Frentanese, a Eucharistic Miracle happened in the little Church of St. Legotian. During the Mass the Host was changed into live FLESH and the wine was changed into live BLOOD.

In 1970-71 and again in 1981 this miracle was put under scientific scrutiny by Professor Odoardo Linoli, eminent Professor in Anatomy and Pathological Histology and in Chemistry and Clinical Microscopy. He was assisted by Professor Ruggero Bertelli of the University of Sienna.

The Host turned to FLESH can be distinctly observed today and its analysis is that the flesh is real flesh and the blood is real blood belonging to the human species.

Another amazing fact is that the FLESH consists of muscular tissue of the heart! The Flesh consists of the muscular tissue of the heart, but not only that, but contains all the parts of the heart - the myocardium, the endocardium, the bags nerve and also the left ventricle of the heart for the large thickness of the myocardium.

The FLESH is a HEART complete in its essential structure!

The preservation of the FLESH and BLOOD remained the same even after twelve centuries exposed to atmospheric and biological agents - an extraordinary phenomenon.

9. Hosts Turn Into Flesh

On August 14, 1730, thieves enters the Church of St. Francis and stole hundreds of consecrated Hosts. Two days later someone discovered a box in another Church in Siena. Priests opened the box and found the missing, stolen Hosts inside entangled in cobwebs and dirt. They were cleaned but not consumed because they were dirty, a priest put them in a sacred place to let age and decompose on their own.

But over the years the Hosts did not deteriorate but appeared fresh and renewed.

The Hosts remains in this state today, 285 years later, and can still be seen in the Basilica of St. Francis in Siena, Italy

10. Bleeding Host

At Saint Mary's parish in Buenos Aires a Host began to bleed during the Mass and became human tissue. A comprehensive study began in 1996 after which the Host was determined to be heart tissue, tissue that had gone through extreme pain.

The bishop who commissioned the study and review of this case was none other than Pope Francis.

11. Host Effusing A Reddish Substance

During Mass at Saint Martin of Tours in Tixtla, Mexico, October 21, 2006, a Host that was to be distributed began to effuse a red substance. The diocese decided to conduct extensive scientific studies to make sure of the cause of the red substance and ensure there was no hoax involved. The study took several years and published in 2013.

The reddish substance was indeed blood of human origin, AB positive, the same type as found another Eucharist miracles and the Holy Shroud of Turin.

Though the blood had coagulated (as expected) there still was Eucharist blood flowing from this living organism with noted white and red blood cells that were active.

12. Host With Face Crowned With Thorns

On April 28, 2001, at Saint Mary in Chirattakonam, India, the Church began the Novena to St. Jude Thaddeus. At 8:49 AM the priest exposed the Most Holy Sacrament in the monstrance for public adoration. After a few minutes three dots appeared in the Holy Eucharist. They prayed to the Host for a while and then placed it in a the secure Tabernacle. (Prayer to the Host is in fact praying to Jesus for the Host IS the body, blood, soul and divinity of Christ).

The priest went to the archbishop and informed him of what had happened. They returned to the Church and looked at the Host that now not only had three red dots, but a face crowned with a crown of thorns.

The Eucharist remains to this day and is often adored by the faithful.

13. Red Spot On The Host

At the Marian Shrine of finca Betania in Cura, Venezuela, on December 8, 1991 the priest had just divided the Host into four parts and consumed on of those pieces. When he placed the remaining pieces on the paten (a plate the host is kept on) he observed that a red dot and from that red dot a red substance coming out, similar in manner to blood coming from a wound. A number o pilgrims there witnessed this and verified that the blood did not come from the priest.

This Host continues to bleed fresh blood to this day.

The Bishop of Los Teques had a series of test done on this Host. The blood, AB positive from a LIVING HEART.

You can go and and see this Host at the convent of the Augustinian Recollects Nuns of the Sacred Heart of Jesus in Los Teques

14. Dirty Host Emits Blood

At a parish Church in Poland, Saint Anthony of Sokolka, on October 12, 2008 a consecrated Host accidentally fell to the ground during Mass. When the priest noticed it, he believed it was dirty so placed it in a vascular (a small container filled with water) so the Host would dissolve in a proper manner.

Later, when the Host was looked at again, it was partially dissolved, but there was what looked like a blood clot in the water. Intense study followed by two scientists of world-wide fame, and other specialists in pathological anatomy at the Medical University of Bialystok including Professor Maria Elzbieta Sobaniec Lotowska and Professor Sulkowski. The two scientists studied the blood clot independent of each other using the most modern optical microscopes and transmission electronic microscope.

To make sure there was no bias, Professor Sulkowski was not informed that he was studying a consecrated Host.

Both scientists came to the same conclusion. There was no blood clot but instead human cardiac muscle tissue and WAS STILL ALIVE!

"Even scientists of NASA, who have at their disposal the most modern analytical techniques, would not be able to artificially recreate such a thing" said Professor Professor Sobaniec-Łotowska.

"Even the scientists of NASA, who have at their disposal the most modern analytical techniques, would not be able to artificially recreate such a thing" affirmed.

We could go on and on and on covering miracle after miracle. But you get the point, don't you? The Eucharist IS NOT just a symbol of Christ, but Christ himself - His FLESH, His BLOOD,

The TOTAL CHRIST.

15

Objections

THOUGH WE HAVE COVERED MOST of the objections in this book, let me list a few of them here. I will not elaborate extensively on any one of them. If you need more information, be sure and read the books I list in the end, books that will go into much more detail on all the subjects I have covered.

1. Jesus is speaking in John 6 figuratively when he said "I am the bread."

This sounds reasonable, doesn't it, since Jesus did speak figuratively on a number of occasions? Look at these figures of speech in John's Gospel: "I am the door, I am the vine, and I am living water."

None of us consider Jesus to be a wooden block of wood like a door or an actual grape vine growing on a hillside. Instead we see what Jesus meant through the symbols and figurative speech he uses. Yet in John 6, we see something totally different.

Jesus not only states that he is the bread of life but repeats it, seeking to drill it into the minds and hearts of those present. Again, and again he repeats the fact about this bread being his FLESH, on and on, making sure they understand what he is saying. There was NO RESISTANCE when he spoke of being water, a door or the vine. Yet here in John 6 the resistance is fierce.

But Jesus doesn't budge or give into their rejection of him being the living bread, FLESH and BLOOD that brings eternal life. Even when most of his followers leave over these direct, shocking statements of his, he does not soften his tone. Why? He means what he says. His words are not to be taken figuratively but literally.

THIS **IS** MY BODY FOR YOU

Jesus shares one of the essentials of becoming a Christian - EAT. Though his words should be understood spiritually ("spirit and life") - these words have great spiritual impact on our lives, they are also to be followed, practiced and believed - eating literally the FLESH and drinking the BLOOD of Jesus Christ the INCARNATE Lord. By this we receive his risen and glorified manhood and also his place in the Trinity so that we can be brought into an eternal fellowship with the Father, Spirit and his incarnate Son.

2. **Sometimes I have heard people say that the Mass is a RE-CRUCIFYING OF JESUS** when in the book of Hebrews it states that he died ONCE AND FOR ALL. Catholics are accused of killing Jesus at every Mass - crucifying and crucifying and crucifying him again and again and again. Is there any truth in this?

Those who make this claim against the Catholic Church are either ignorant or they are seeking to deceive their followers. How can a claim like this against the Catholic Church have any traction when it goes counter to clear Catholic teaching? The Church DOES NOT re-crucify Jesus at every Mass.
Then what do they do on the altar?

It's simple. They bring that ONE CRUCIFIXION of Jesus into the present. They don't re-crucify Jesus again and again and again. That is nonsense. Those who teach that the Catholic Church does this are being dishonest. Read the Catechism of the Catholic Church. The teaching is clear.

Then, why an altar at all? It is to bring this ONCE AND FOR ALL SACRIFICE into the present, a non-bloody sacrifice so that the bread becomes his saving FLESH and the wine his saving BLOOD, given as a remission for our sin, to wash them away by the power of God's forgiveness.

3. **Often Fundamentalist, Evangelical and main stream Protestants love to quote John 6:63**, thinking that this verse ends all debate as to whether the bread becomes the actual FLESH of Jesus and the wine his BLOOD.

Notice what John 6:63 says:

It is the spirit that gives life, the flesh is of no avail; the words I have spoken to you are spirit and life.

Ah. They think they have us Catholics with this verse, reciting it with a smile. They say that it proves that when Jesus talked about FLESH it meant nothing, or to drink Jesus' BLOOD would be a waste of time.

Now let me ask you, if you know anything about Biblical interpretation, does that make sense? Here Jesus has laid down a metric that must be followed: "Eat my FLESH and drink my BLOOD if you want to have eternal life." It's clear, isn't it?

For a person to use John 6:63 to discount all that Jesus did and said sounds absurd. But many Protestants do it. They use this verse to wipe away all the bold statements Jesus is saying, all the radical ways to find eternal food and life through eating the eternal bread (FLESH) and drinking the eternal life-giving liquid (BLOOD).

They MUST DO IT or become Catholic. If pastors interpreted John 6 literally they would have to leave their churches. If churches did the same, they would either have to close or see if they could be turned into Catholic places of worship.

You see why there is so much attention to John 6, don't you? You either have to accept what Jesus said or somehow find a way to deny it.

And John 6:63 is their way around it.

So, if one wants to be honest and find out the true meaning of John 6:63, how should he approach the verse?

Let's look at the word FLESH. Jesus uses it enough times in this passage for us to know what he means. He talks about bread (of course he had feed the crowd with miracle bread). Now he talks about the bread from heaven WHICH IS HIS FLESH. He then goes on to state boldly that they must eat his FLESH if they want to have eternal life.

For us to interpret Jesus words: "the flesh counts for nothing" can't ever refer to the long preceding dialogue Jesus gave about eating his FLESH and drinking his BLOOD to FIND ETERNAL LIFE. Are we saying that eternal life counts for nothing? Or are we concluding that the way to gain eternal life by eating the FLESH and BLOOD of Christ counts for nothing? Are you kidding? This would be nonsense!

In John 6:63 Jesus is using the word FLESH in a totally different way than he used before. In this verse it is obviously referring to the FALLEN FLESH, that kind unaided by the Spirit, diminished and darkened by sin.

In fact, those who were following him and then turned aside because of what he said about consuming his FLESH and BLOOD were following their own fleshly thoughts, unaided by the Holy Spirit.

You see, the things Jesus was declaring could ONLY BE UNDERSTOOD BY THE SPIRIT - not the flesh. This is why Jesus said that the words he spoke to them about eating HIM were so deep, so spiritual that it would take the Holy Spirit to understand them.

By using the term "spirit" he was not saying that what he said about eating his FLESH and drinking his BLOOD were not be taken literally. No! Instead these bold, radical statements of Jesus CAN ONLY BE UNDERSTAND BY MEANS OF THE HOLY SPIRIT. If you are not guided by him, you will run away like his followers did.

And that is what all Protestants are doing - running away from what Jesus declared. It is beyond their understanding. What they need is to settle their hearts and minds, pull back from all their indoctrination as Protestants and let the Spirit teach them.

The flesh will move them away from Christ. The Spirit will draw them into the net of faith, captured by Jesus, and willing to come and drink of eternal life.

St. Paul clearly teaches this when he says:

The cup of blessing which we bless, is it not a *PARTICIPATION* IN THE BLOOD OF CHRIST? The bread which we break, is it not a *PARTICIPATION* IN THE BODY OF CHRIST?

I Cor. 10:16

So when we take communion we are not just consuming symbols but the actual FLESH and BLOOD of Christ.

Could it be that anyone who denies that Jesus comes in the flesh in the Eucharist is believing a lie promoted by the antichrist - in fact these

Christians who only believe in the Spiritual part of communion and deny the incarnational part have the spirit of antiChrist?

Amazing!   Thanks be to God for his unspeakable, timeless gift!

4. **Another objection that I heard when I attended Dallas Theological Seminary** seemed to settle the question about the statement, "This is my body, this is my blood...". The professor said that one can't take it literally since he hadn't been crucified yet. Therefore it had to be a symbol.

    This does seem to be a reasonable objection until you read that Jesus was "slain from the foundation of the world." (Revelation 13:8). So when Jesus held up the bread and said: "This is my body..." he could actual say it because he, in God's time, (and who understands that!) had already been crucified.

    So don't use time as an argument to prove the words of Jesus are only a symbol.

    Jesus did not say: "This will be my body, but IS my body." And even if you want to interpret

Revelation 13:8 in a way that will not support my argument, Jesus, being the all powerful God could, at his word, create his true flesh even as his words created the universe and all that is.

Don't ever doubt the power of God to do the impossible. That's his niche - doing things that are beyond our comprehension, even creating flesh out of bread before the historical event actually occurred (though already occurring in the mind, plan and purpose of God long before the world was created).

Is what I wrote hard to grasp. Of course. None of us understand the basic component parts of the universe - matter, time and space. So why do we think that we can understand this great miracle of the Eucharist, a sacrament associated with matter, time and space.

5. **When I bring up a topic like what is covered in book I often hear this reply: "Let's not argue about all this stuff.** All we need to do is believe in and follow Jesus. Don't bring up all these things that divide us?"

Sounds good doesn't it? Be nice. Be agreeable. Be kind and irenic. Don't be so opinionated!

Well, we all should, as Christians, be kind and loving to each other.   Yet when another Christian is denying a CENTRAL TRUTH of the Church, we are obligated to talk and write about it.

And listen. That statement, "I just want to be a Christian," is often a way to AVOID study, research, heart searching questions of ones own faith and practice.

Yes, we want to be Christians who get along, but how can we support each other if we deny the clear teaching of Jesus Christ? Am I to let people believe and practice heresy or should I call them on it? Isn't it loving to point people to the truth and encourage them to walk in it?

Of course.

There is no doubt that I just want to be a Christian.   Yet in saying this, I want to be a Christian that fully follows the TRUTH, particularly when it is a central truth that is essential to my faith.

16

One Last Word

LET ME COVER THE ESSENTIAL POINTS I have broached in this book. Understand me, I mean what I say when I say that Protestants only get the God side of Christ and not the Man side because they do not receive the true FLESH and BLOOD of Christ - his incarnational being - THE MAN CHRIST JESUS. Because of this they are only getting ½ of Jesus not the TOTAL JESUS.

This is not just a casual thing, but very serious. When anyone does not follow a CLEAR TEACHING of Christ as found in John 6, (As well as St. Paul in Corinthians 10-11) they are in rebellion. Now, most Protestants are not in active rebellion but in passive rebellion. Many do not know at all that they have not received the TOTAL CHRIST.

As a pastor, I didn't know.

There is so much ignorance. And that is sad. Here Jesus offers HIMSELF, fully, totally, and many Christians never come to receive the gift - the TOTAL GIFT of the incarnational Christ - the MAN, the GOD. They receive Christ spiritually but never physically. And it's a requirement for eternal life!

I believe that God will forgive you if you are ignorant. But if you WILLFULLY REJECT THE TOTAL CHRIST you are putting your soul in jeopardy.

That's serious!

I would encourage you to go back and underline parts of this book you don't understand. Read these parts prayerfully.

You will be tempted to run to a favorite pastor or theologian and see what they say. You already know. They will despise what I have taught in this book - some even saying that we worship a piece of bread and a goblet of wine.

It is true that we worship the bread - the BREAD OF LIFE, and the wine - BLOOD OF CHRIST shed for the remission of sins. In worshipping the consecrated elements we are worshipping Jesus

Christ. It is either him or not. The Holy Scriptures clearly teach that the BREAD and the WINE are in fact JESUS CHRIST the incarnate one - the God Man who gives his life for us.

Why reject it?

My prayer is that you will come boldly, eat and drink freely at the Table set up for you, that Eucharist Table that contains what Ponce de Leon desired - something to bring life that will have no end.

He didn't find it.

You can.

You know right where to get it...at your local Catholic Church.[18]

---

[18]Don't rush in and receive this life-giving elements of communion until you talk with a Priest. He will guide so that you can be prepared for this great and sacred event.

The following few pages contain a brochure that we used at my Church. I wrote it to emphasize the unique character of the Catholic Church and the food we serve - bread and wine, the body and blood of Christ our Savior.

Come.
Eat.
Drink.
Savor.
The Savior
Our eternal food.

After all, you are what you eat.

How long has it been since you were served the BEST FOOD ever?

...I mean really good food - food that totally satisfies?

YOU WON'T BELIEVE... where you can find it!

It's at your local Catholic Church, possibly the one you once attended.

I know what you're thinking. "THE CATHOLIC CHURCH?"

"Is there good food there?"

Well, the best food in the world is served daily at your local Catholic Church.

You see, we all have our favorite foods.

Some Italian. Who can't pass up great pizza or a variety of pasta dishes?

And there is Mexican, French, German, good ole American cuisine, and so many others.

Great stuff!

But nothing compares to the meal you get at the Catholic Church.

NOTHING!

Oh I know...

Some of you have given up on the Catholic Church...

...all the problems you read about with priests, boring homilies, time away from what you really like to do - golf, football, being outdoors, reading, gardening, and so many other things...that crowd your time.

And that all leads to a hunger that you are not satisfying, an INNER ACHE that will not go away...

No matter what you do or what you buy.

YOU LONG AND HUNGER FOR TRUE JOY that bubbles up from inside...

Chasing away the depression, the feelings of uselessness and the lack of recognition that eats away at your inner self.

YOU DREAM OF A PEACE that frees you from all that anxiety you feel...

The stress, the feelings that life is passing you by and you are missing out on what it means to really live.

Food. Hunger. SATISFYING THAT INNER HUNGER.

It can all happen at your local Catholic Church.

How?

At every Mass, the bread and wine are transformed into the body and blood of Christ. His life becomes food.

And it is the BEST FOOD you could ever receive.

How's that?

Jesus – God himself, is actually taken into your inner self.

You see, when God made you, he set aside a special place for himself in your inner self – your soul.

TOO MANY TRY TO FILL THAT GOD-SHAPED VACUUM WITH EVERYTHING BUT GOD. We all do that.

That's why we suffer from those feelings of anxiety, stress, depression, inadequacy, resentment, fear and so many other feelings that swamp our souls.

But get this! When you begin to take in the right food for your soul – the life of God found in Jesus, that empty place begins to feel nourished, satisfied...

WHOLE!

So what can you do about it?

Go to the Catholic Church this Sunday. You may feel a little out of place, but that's OK.

Come, sing, pray, open your soul, and receive Christ in the bread and wine.[19]

You may not feel the difference immediately. But you will ultimately feel a satisfaction in your inner being that you have not felt in a long time.

It's the food you need. The BEST FOOD in the world!

Saint Hubert Catholic Church

A Friendly, Faith-filled Church

804 3rd St. Langley, WA
(360) 221-5383

Mass Times

Saturday 5:00 pm
Sunday 8:00.10:30, 10:30 am
And other daily masses

Come as you are...
You'll be loved!

Pastor: Fr. Rick Spicer

---

[19] First, talk to a priest to better help you understand how to receive this food from God - this heavenly manna for your soul.

17

Your Next Step

Since you have taken the time to read this book, **why not visit a local Catholic Church.** If you have a Cathedral around you, go there and prayerfully observe.

As you walk in, you will notice a red candle in a glass vase that's lit. It signals that CONSECRATED HOSTS are in the Tabernacle (a place where the sacred bread is kept).
This means that
JESUS IS PRESENT
in a special way.

149

Not that he is not always present (omniscient) but rather that he is also *particularly present* in HIS BODY - HIS FLESH.

Kneel and drink it in. It may be foreign to you, but what you see represents what the Church has been doing for thousands of years.

After this, find a Catholic Church that has an
Adoration Room
where there is an Exposition of the Most Holy Eucharist (consecrated) and placed in a Monstrance (a special vessel)
in which the consecrated Host is exposed for the adoration of the faithful.
You will discover that this place is one of great holiness and reverence.

Kneel.

Pray.

Let this experience
of being in the visible
presence of Jesus
sink deep into your soul.

You will not be the same!

18

Books For Further Study and Research

The Hidden Manna: A Theology of the Eucharist
James T. O'Connor

Eucharistic Miracles
Joan Carroll Cruz

The Eucharist: A Bible Study Guide for Catholics
Mitch Pacwa

Jesus and the Jewish Roots of the Eucharist: Unlocking the Secrets of the Last Supper
Brant Pitre

Symbol or Substance? A Dialogue on the Eucharist with C. S. Lewis, Billy Graham and J. R. R. Tolkien
Peter Kreeft

This Is My Body: An Evangelical Discovers the Real Presence
Mark P. Shea

The Lamb's Supper: The Mass as Heaven on Earth
Scott Hahn

Books by Dave Armstrong: Dave Armstrong's Catholic Apologetics Bookstore: 50 Books. Great Catholic apologist and former Protestant Evangelical.

In the Presence of Our Lord, the History, Theology, and Psychology of Eucharistic Devotion
Father Benedict J. Groeschel, C.F.R., and James Monti

The Case for Catholicism : Answers to Classic and Contemporary Protestant Objections
Trent Horn

Surprised by Truth (3 vols)
Patrick Madrid

This series is awesome! You will read the accounts of other Protestants who became Catholics, many pastors who were Protestant.

Rome Sweet Home
Scott and Kimberly Haun
Protestants who struggled with becoming Catholic.

Crossing the Tiber
Evangelical Protestants Discover the Historical Church
Steve Ray

For an array of stories of Protestants who became Catholic - see the **Coming Home Network (chnetwork.org)** and also **Catholic Answers catholic.com** for great materials.

Many of those who wrote these books were former Protestant Evangelicals….AMAZING! Many risked their jobs, marriages, and standing within their group to become Catholic.

Why?

The TRUTH set them **free!**

FREE BOOKS
For
YOU!

Be sure and go to <u>DrPaulYoung.com</u> and sign up for a **free book**, a book designed to take you to a new level in your walk with God.

And keep watching this site because new free books will be offered periodically.

Last, **pray for our ministry**. We are seeking to change the hearts and souls of thousands of people around the world and need your prayers. Send me a note at <u>pauljyoung@mac.com</u> if you will pray for us.

Thanks, and God bless you!

Dr. Paul J. Young

Education:

University of California, Fresno, B.A in English

Dallas Theological Seminary, Th.M (Masters in Theology)

Biola University, Doctorate of Ministry with emphasis on psychology (working with Talbot School of Theology, Rosemead School of Psychology and other schools). Dr. Young's Doctoral degree is not in Clinical Psychology but rather in Pastoral Psychology.

Dr. Paul Joseph Young

Dr. Young helped grow one of the largest churches in the Dallas/Ft. Worth area as its pastor, working with thousands of people, developing his skills both as a minister, theologian, communicator and a counselor (pastoral psychology), working with hundreds of people and developing his unique therapy techniques.

For seven years he was C.E.O. of Community Bible Study International, working in over 60 countries of the world, sharing his message of truth, hope and joy. He held seminars on anxiety, anxiety, stress, fear, anger, and a host of other topics, seeking to bring healing to the thousands in need.

Dr. Paul's communication skills has made him a favorite speaker around the world. He lives with his wife and best friend, Diane. They have five children and 14 grandchildren.

More than anything, Dr. Paul lives to help people find the joyful, peaceful life they deserve.

This is a

DrPaulYoung.com

Publication

Made in the USA
Columbia, SC
24 October 2020